Patterns at the
SEASHORE

by Dawn Bluemel Oldfield

Consultant: Kimberly Brenneman, PhD
National Institute for Early Education Research, Rutgers University
New Brunswick, New Jersey

BEARPORT
PUBLISHING

New York, New York

Credits

Cover, © Claudia Paulussen/Shutterstock; 3, © Gregory Guivarch/Shutterstock; 4, © StacieStauffSmith Photos/Shutterstock; 4–5, © MaszaS/Shutterstock; 6–7, © Shutterstock; 8–9, © AzureRepublicPhotography/Alamy; 10–11, © Jorge Moro/Shutterstock; 12–13, © Kim Ruoff/Thinkstock; 14–15, © OpopO/Shutterstock; 16, © Wolfgang Poelzer; 17, © Dirk Wiersma; 18–19, © Michael Wick/Shutterstock; 20–21, © Wolta/Shutterstock; 22–23, © Karen Wunderman; 24–25, © robertdewit66/Thinkstock; 26–27, © Cigdem Sean Cooper; 28, © Kenneth Keifer; 29, © Dennis Mook/SuperStock/Corbis; 30A, © Francisco Javier Herrero Isla; 30B, © Myrmidon/Shutterstock; 30C, © Krzysztof Odziomek/Shutterstock; 30D, © Kameel4u/Shutterstock; 31TL, © AzureRepublicPhotography/Alamy; 31TR, © Ariel Bravy/Shutterstock; 31BL, © Wolta/Shutterstock; 31BR, © MrKornFlakes/Thinkstock.

Publisher: Kenn Goin
Senior Editor: Joyce Tavolacci
Creative Director: Spencer Brinker
Design: Debrah Kaiser
Photo Researcher: We Research Pictures, LLC.

Library of Congress Cataloging-in-Publication Data

Bluemel Oldfield, Dawn, author.
   Patterns at the seashore / by Dawn Bluemel Oldfield.
      pages cm. — (Seeing patterns all around)
   Includes bibliographical references and index.
   ISBN-13: 978-1-62724-335-3 (library binding : alk. paper)
   ISBN-10: 1-62724-335-6 (library binding : alk. paper)
   1. Pattern perception—Juvenile literature. 2. Shapes—Juvenile literature. 3. Seashore—Juvenile literature. I. Title.
   BF294.B58 2015
   516.15—dc23
                              2014009093

For more information, write to Bearport Publishing Company, Inc., 45 West 21st Street, Suite 3B, New York, New York 10010. Printed in the United States of America.

10 9 8 7 6 5 4 3 2 1

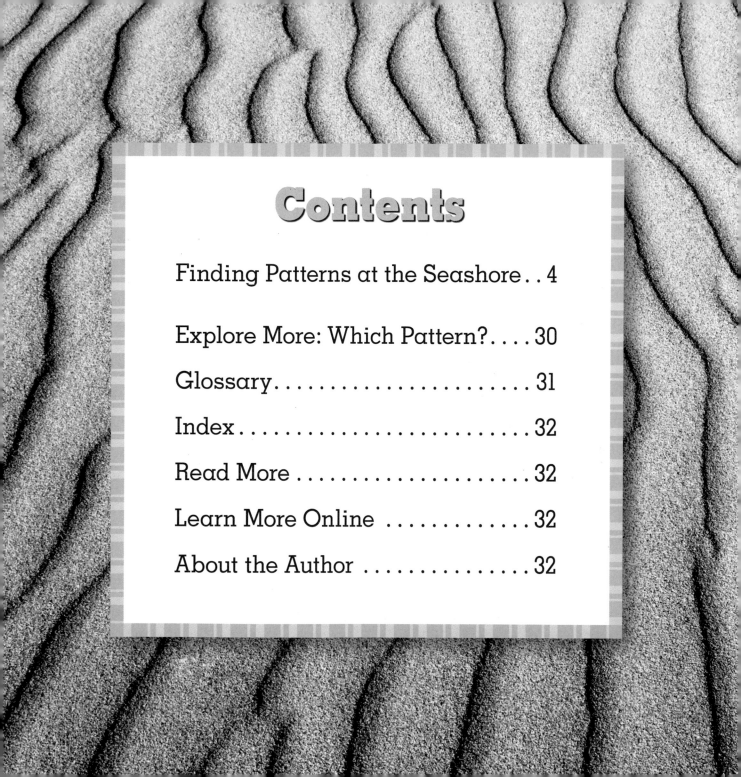

Contents

Finding Patterns at the Seashore

Patterns can be shapes, colors, or sizes that repeat.

You can see patterns at the seashore.

A row of sand castles makes a pattern.

5

Fish swimming in the sea make a pattern.

Big, small.

The pattern repeats.

One stripe is not a pattern.

It does not repeat.

However, many stripes on chairs make a pattern.

Red, white.

The colors repeat.

They make an **alternating** pattern.

Flip-flops in the sand
make a colorful pattern.

10

Yellow, blue, pink, green.

The pattern repeats.

White circles on a blue dress make a pattern of dots.

They are called polka dots.

13

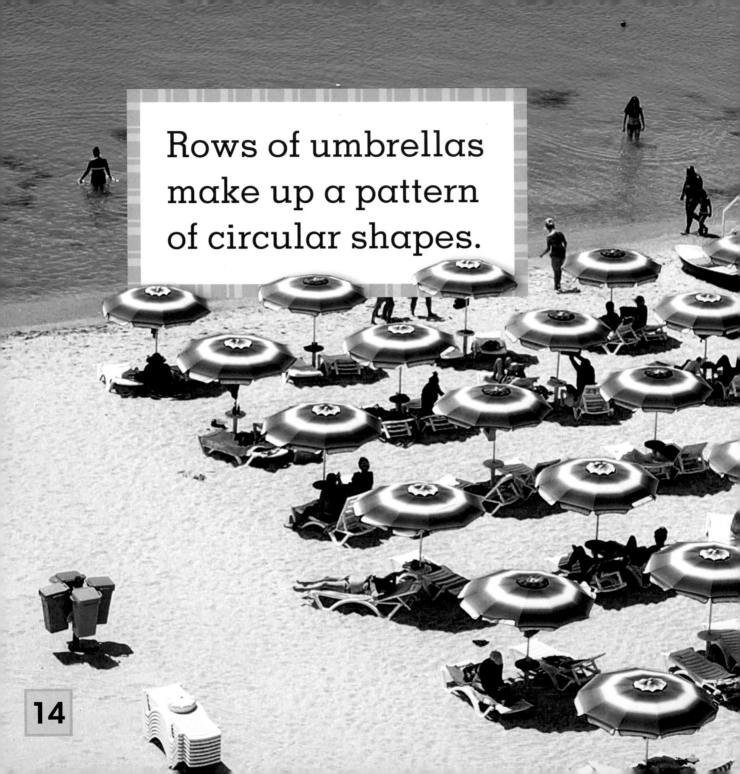

Rows of umbrellas make up a pattern of circular shapes.

Patterns can go round and round.

Snail shells have a **spiral** pattern.

snail

17

Beach balls have a colorful pattern.

Blue, white, yellow, white, red, white.

This pattern appears on each ball.

An eel hunts for food.

Its black spots are different shapes and sizes.

This makes an **irregular pattern**.

Four pelicans face different directions on a **dock**.

The birds form a pattern.

Right, left.

Round holes in the dock make another pattern!

The holes go on and on.

Some patterns include
different shapes.

This whale shark's skin
has white dots and lines.

They repeat over the
fish's body.

Patterns can be small.

The shape of a scale repeats on a fish's body.

The fish's scales make a pattern.

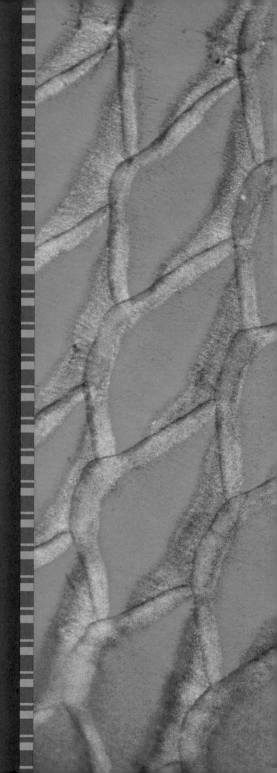

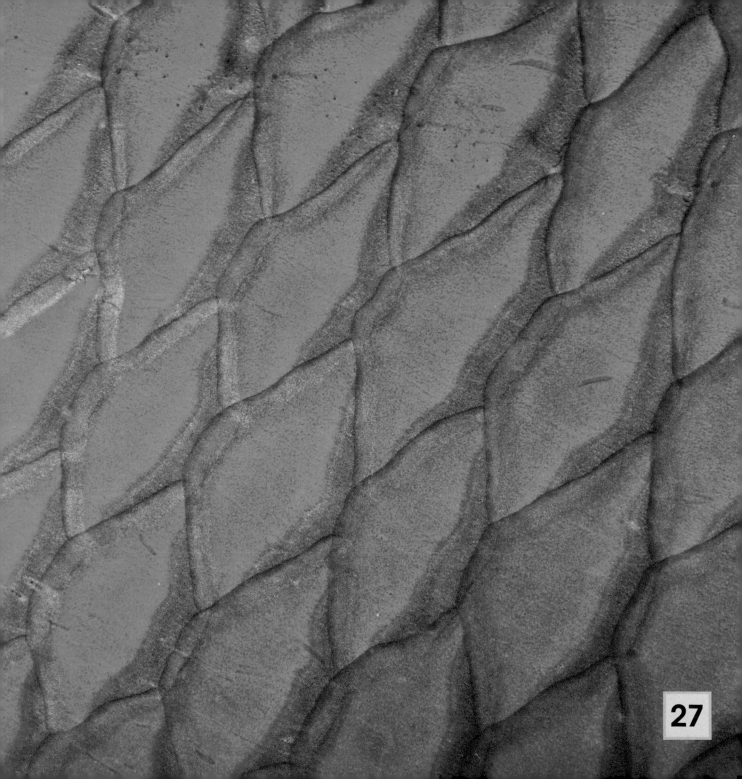

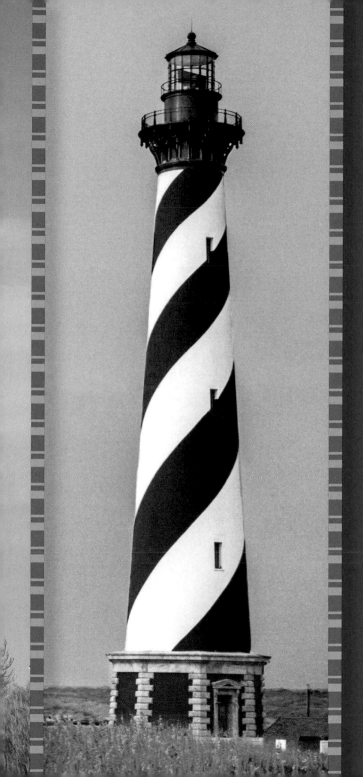

A lighthouse is a tall building with a light at the top.

What patterns do you see on these lighthouses?

Patterns are everywhere!

Explore More:
Which Pattern?

Look at the pictures. Each one shows a kind of pattern that can be found at the seashore. Match each pattern with the correct picture.

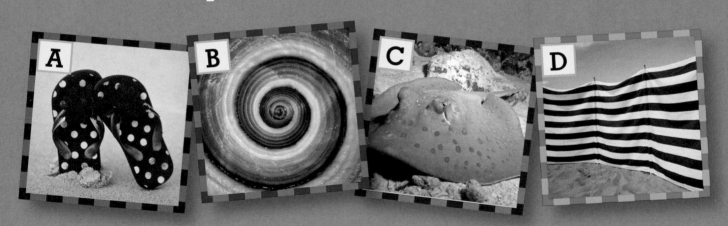

A

B

C

D

1. spiral pattern

2. alternating pattern

3. irregular pattern

4. polka dot pattern

Answers are on page 32.

Glossary

alternating (AWL-tur-*nayt*-ing) changing back and forth, such as between two colors

dock (DOK) a landing area where ships load and unload goods

irregular pattern (ih-REG-yuh-lur PAT-urn) a pattern that has one or more similar parts unequal in size, shape, or in the way they are arranged

spiral (SPYE-ruhl) winding or circling around a center

Index

Read More

Harris, Trudy. *Pattern Fish*. Minneapolis, MN: Millbrook Press (2000).

Nunn, Daniel. *Patterns Outside (Math Every Day)*. Chicago: Raintree (2012).

Learn More Online

To learn more about patterns at the seashore, visit
www.bearportpublishing.com/SeeingPatternsAllAround

About the Author

Dawn Bluemel Oldfield is a freelance writer. When she isn't writing, she enjoys reading, traveling, and working in her garden, where there are patterns in many shapes and colors. She and her husband live in Prosper, Texas.

Answers for Page 30:

1. B; 2. D; 3. C; 4. A

32